ANDY
ABRAHAM

ANDY
ABRAHAM
REMEMBER
WHEN...

COMPACT
disc

C000126325

REMEMBER
WHEN...

ANDY ABRAHAM

REMEMBER WHEN...

First Published in the UK in 2012 by EJ Entertainments Ltd

Printed and Bound in China

© Champions (UK) PLC
www.championsukplc.com

Packaged for Champions (UK) PLC by Instinctive Product Development Ltd
www.instinctivepd.com

ISBN: 978-1-907657-96-2

Written by Andy Abraham with Richard Havers

Designed by: BrainWave

Cover design by: Champions (UK) PLC

Images courtesy of PA Photos, Champions (UK) PLC, Anthony Stanley of STF Photo Agency and The Dicks Archive

ANDY
ABRAHAM

REMEMBER
WHEN....

RememberWhen

I've always wanted to do a collection of songs that have been important and influential to me. The cover versions on this album are in most cases an integral part of the fabric of my life. Each one of them taps into an area of my emotional well, reminding me of things that have happened, my friends and the times that have helped to make me the person that I am.

I didn't just want to do a collection of any old covers – it had to be a collection of songs that were very important to me. Each one brings back specific memories – memories of growing up, people that have gone, people that are still here, people that I love and artists that have inspired and shaped me as a singer and as a human being. This is music that has made me conscious of the world and touched me in a way that makes me want to own each and every one of the songs that I sing.

The first ten songs on this album, the cover versions, are songs of my soul. Rather than just singing the songs and leaving you to guess how and why they might be important to me, I wanted to have the space to explain why they are very special. I've tried to perform them like

"I just hope that you love these songs as much as I do."

it was the first time anybody had ever heard them, like I had written them and presented them to the world for the first time.

It has been such an honour to sing these songs from writers and performers that have spiritually lifted me up and taken me to a place which brings back great memories for me – whether they be happy, sad or joyous. Above all else every single one of those songs make me want to never forget who I am and why I am the way I am. If these songs make you *Remember When*, in the way that I remember when, then I will have succeeded. That's the power of music – the power of song – it can hit you when you're up and it can hit you when you're down; you just never know how it will hit you. These are the songs of my soul that I'm singing for you.

I feel very blessed and very honoured to be able to sing these songs for you. It's been an emotional ride recalling these memories but it was a journey well worth taking.

Andy Abraham
x xx

Like the rest of the country during the autumn of 2005 I was glued to my TV set watching *The X Factor*. At the time I said to friends and to people I was working with, "Wow! Andy Abraham has an amazing voice." Little did I know we would get the opportunity to work together six years later, just as I was preparing to appear on *The X Factor* as its Director of Artiste Development. Then again, as we all know, God moves in mysterious ways…

I've always believed that music carries us to a place – a place where our imagination takes over. Through the power of music we can share our most intimate moments, often in unimaginable ways – sometimes with complete strangers. From birth to death, a first kiss, a first dance, a new home, a marriage and the times of heart-breaking situations, music helps to shape our lives. Music reminds us of who we are and it touches our soul.

When Andy started to tell me the reasons for choosing these particular songs I was touched by the intensity of his feelings for them, the way that they reminded him of happy times, of sad times and how these songs are like a musical autobiography. It's why we decided to accompany Andy's new recording with his words and photographs from his life. It felt like the best way of allowing everyone to better get to know Andy, while at the same time listening to one of Britain's best singers.

I've been lucky enough to have had No.1 singles, walked the red carpet, to have been nominated for a Golden Globe and had the highest ever British entry in the US charts. And while the walls of my studio are full of platinum and gold discs I remain humbled by the power of music.

I hope you enjoy listening to Andy's songs, reading about why he chose them and sharing in the life of one of the nicest, and most talented, singers I've had the privilege to work with.

Eliot Kennedy

"Everyone has a story, and the soundtrack is song."

"Music really does make a difference to our world."

For the
GoodTimes

Andy's influences – **Perry Como & Al Green**

I was born Andrew Abraham Campbell – the reason for my middle name now being my surname is that it was my dad's name. Of course there's nothing unusual about being named after your father; it is something that happens in many families, but my mum called me that to ensure I had a connection to my dad that would last a lifetime, for both her and for me as tragically, six months before I was born, my mother lost her soul mate – the love of her life – my father.

It was Christmas 1963 that my father passed away and it's one of my greatest regrets that I didn't get to know him. Mum and Dad had already had my big sister Judy, although not much bigger as Mum became pregnant with me within a few months of my sister being born. Mum and Dad were planning to get married but he died before they got the chance. It was such a cruel trick for life to play on my mum, although when I was a kid I didn't understand any of that. Later on, even after she married my stepfather, I could tell by the way she spoke of my dad that she loved him so very much.

Not only did Mum have to cope with the loss of my dad, she also had a real problem with me when I was born in July 1964. I was very ill and spent the first ten months of my life in hospital. I had severe

Me and my big sister. As a kid I couldn't understand how come I had three hands! ▶
Perry Como was always an inspiration. ▶▶

"My mum would put this song on and my sister and I would dance to it in the front room."

11

gastroenteritis and was given the last rites on several occasions. Mum was so worried for me, especially having already lost my father – she was determined to keep me; she needed me to be her link with what might have been. Even from a very young age Mum said she could see my dad in me – my facial expressions, my attitude and my humour.

That's where my connection and love for this song comes from. Mum loved music and she loved Al Green's singing and it was his version of the song that she would have heard for the first time when I was about six years old. I heard it too, but it was only as I got a little older that it lodged in my brain and I understood the powerful message that Mum was hearing in the lyrics. Once I began to appreciate great singers, Al Green was one of my first loves. If it were only just our family's love for his singing the song then it would be deserving of its place among the songs that have shaped my life, but there's a twist, perhaps of fate, that makes it the perfect song to open my album.

Perry Como's version of the song was a favourite of my wife Denise's parents; she's from an Irish Catholic family and when I first started dating Denise and we used to go up to see her family at Morecambe in Lancashire we would have sing-songs at which everyone would be allocated a song to sing – Denise's mum and dad would choose *For the Good Times*.

It's strange that the two families, so far apart, one up in Morecambe and one down in London, both loved the same song. When Denise's dad passed away I was asked to sing this song at his graveside. It was one of the hardest things I've had to do as a singer, but also very lovely to do something like that for a very special family. When I was recording it in the studio I was thinking of Denise's dad, my mum and of course my dad. I can tell that it was an emotionally charged session for me.

My mum Agatha Campbell with Denise's mum & dad, Patrick & Bridie Harkin, walking at Morecambe Bay with my tiny tots Tara & Jacob (who's out of shot in the push chair). ▶

"There's two reasons for choosing this song. My mum loved Al Green's version and Denise's mum and dad loved Perry Como singing *For the Good Times.*"

For the **Good Times**

Written by Kris Kristofferson in 1970

Perry Como's single made No.7 on the UK charts (1973).
Al Green from his album, *I'm Still in Love With You* (1972).

Kris Kristofferson's version appeared on his debut album and was one of four standout tracks that included *Me and Bobby McGhee*, *Help Me Make It Through the Night* and *Sunday Mornin' Comin' Down*. The first cover version of *For the Good Times* was by Ray Price and his version topped the country music charts in America and was awarded the accolade of Song of the Year by the Academy of Country Music. It was soon covered by a whole host of other artists including Elvis Presley and Isaac Hayes.

Perry Como's version was not a hit in America but proved very popular in Britain. Perry had started out as a boy singer with the big bands in the 1930s. He, like Frank Sinatra, left the big bands in the early 1940s to forge a career as a solo singer and it wasn't long before he was having hit records with a huge following among the 'bobby-soxers'. Between 1943 and 1954 Perry had over 80 hit recordings on the *Billboard* singles chart, including 11 No.1s. Between 1955 and 1974, the year in which he had his last hit record, he had 50 more hits including three No.1s of which the best known is probably *Catch A Falling Star*. Como's relaxed style was popular not just on record but also on his long-running TV shows in America that also aired in Britain.

Like Perry Como, Al Green was a really smooth singer, albeit of soul records rather than more traditional ballads. Southern soul singers have always had one foot in country music so Al Green's cover of *For the Good Times* was a natural step as he searched for the right kind of material for his fourth album for Hi Records.

Kris Kristofferson. ◀

BornFree

Andy's influence – Matt Monro

I didn't always want to be a singer; when I was very young I had my heart set on becoming a vet. I loved insects and bugs and anything to do with the outdoors. One day my mum took me to see the film, *Born Free*, because of my love for nature. When I came out of the cinema I couldn't stop singing the song. I loved it so much that I kept asking my mum to buy the record for me; she eventually did, just to shut me up. Then I played it non-stop.

Whenever I hear the song on the radio it reminds me of being really happy and loving life. I think it's the connection to the film, of watching something so young grow into a graceful creature and then being allowed to run free. In some subconscious way I think I thought that it was me.

Even from a very young age I had thoughts of running free, so much so that my mum had to have eyes in the back of her head to keep me under control. On one occasion I frightened my mother very badly, although I was too young to realise what I was doing.

We were living in East London at the time, which was a pretty rough area. We lived on an estate, a very close knit estate, and I always remember these early years as a very happy time for us as a family. One day I was playing with my toy car outside on the balcony of our fourth-storey flat. I decided to throw the car over the side so that I could watch it fall all the way to the ground. Mum was cleaning up in the flat and I said, "I'm just going to get my car". To be fair I'm not sure if she even heard me, so I ventured down the stairs and picked up my car. Having done so another brainwave struck me, if you can call it such a thing. I thought to myself, I'm going to go to the pictures and I headed off down the street. I was three years old.

Maybe I had *Born Free* in my mind, but I was definitely roaming free and on my way. I'd probably got about two miles from home when a police car went past me. It pulled up, turned around and came back, stopping beside me so the policeman could open his window to talk to me. "Hello young man, where are you going?" "I'm going to the pictures!" I replied, as bold as you like.

"Well you better jump in the car and we'll take you to the pictures." Without hesitating

Where I used to live, Leaside House. ▶

"I bet my doing this song surprises a few people."

I did just that and we drove off down the road. Of course they didn't take me to the pictures, instead we went straight to the police station where they put me in a room filled with loads of toys. I was in my element and soon forgot all about my great adventure. How long I was there I'm not sure but I remember I was enjoying myself and I guess it was a couple of hours later that my mum turned up.

Instead of being cross with me she was just overjoyed that I was safe and sound. Years later she told me how she was going from door to door asking our neighbours if they had seen me or knew what had happened to me. In the end she decided to phone the police station; as a parent myself I can well imagine what was going through her mind. She was worried sick. But as is obvious, the story had a happy ending. She certainly kept a closer eye on me after that although my spirit of adventure remained all through my teens.

During my years at junior school my love of animals, flies and spiders continued. I was always getting hold of a bottle and putting bugs into it so I could watch them run around. Television programmes about nature and survival always captured my imagination and by the time I was around ten or 11 I didn't just want to be a vet, I wanted to be a vet at London Zoo.

I had my heart set on going to London Zoo to help out, checking out the animals and doing odd jobs. My mum sent a letter to them asking if it would be possible for me to visit and do just that. They replied saying it was completely out of the question and at the time it really knocked the ambition out of me.

While it may surprise some people that I'm singing *Born Free*, it shouldn't. My first album was called *The Impossible Dream* after the Andy Williams song that I covered. It also featured *When I Fall In Love* and *Unforgettable*, two songs made famous by Nat King Cole. When I first had the idea of becoming a singer it wasn't just soul music that I listened to, it was singers like Matt Monro, Nat King Cole, Frankie Laine and Frank Sinatra. All these wonderful singers taught me so much but *Born Free* is the song from this era that will always have a special place in my heart.

Virginia McKenna and Bill Travers with the three lion cubs who appear in the film *Born Free*. ▶

Born **Free**

Written by John Barry (music) & Don Black (words) in 1966

It was not a hit single at the time but became Matt Monro's signature tune for the remainder of his career.

Matt Monro's first hit record was his biggest, at least as far as the charts were concerned, although he was not the kind of singer who should really be judged on chart success – he was way better than that. *Portrait of My Love* was that first hit and it reached No.3 on the charts in early 1961.

Over the next three or four years the former bus driver and singer with the BBC Showband charted numerous records, but none did very well. To be fair, the people buying records at that point were interested in different kinds of singers. His version of *Softly As I Leave You* got to No.10; it's a song that Frank Sinatra also recorded and for many people Matt's version is superior, which tells you something about how good he was. In 1963 he recorded the theme song to the Bond movie, *From Russia With Love*, which is the song he is probably best remembered for, despite the fact that it only got to No.20. *Born Free* won an Academy Award for best original song in a movie.

He continued making fabulous records and appeared all over the world in concert and cabaret before dying tragically young in 1985 at just 54. Matt Monro was often called the 'Singer's singer' – well he should be everyone's singer.

Matt Monro. ◀

Mercy

MercyMe

(The Ecology)

Andy's influence – Marvin Gaye

From the moment I first heard him sing I became a fan of Marvin Gaye. It was his album *What's Going On* that first turned me on to his fabulous voice and his amazing song writing. It came out in 1971 and it was when I was a teenager that a friend played it to me; I was immediately hooked on both the music and the message. Besides *Mercy Mercy Me* there's the title track, which quickly became a favourite of mine too. From this album I found *Let's Get it On* which came out in 1976 and is another classic record; there is also *Come Get To This*, which is fabulous.

But it was more than just the great music that Marvin Gaye gave to the world. He also spread a message of tolerance that these albums addressed – especially on *What's Going On*. For me it has never mattered if someone is black or white; it didn't matter whether or not someone had long hair or short hair, it has always been about living life and respecting everybody. It's also about being conscious of who you are, of not abusing your fellow man and about what damage we are doing to the earth.

Of course I was aware from a young age of my colour and never more so than when I got my first car. I would often get pulled up by the police, which made me feel like a statistic as well as making me angry. Yet at the same time my mum wanted me to marry a good black girl – a nice Grenadian or a West Indian girl – which shows another side to prejudice.

Maybe I was lucky because even from my very earliest memories, my life was filled with people from all over the world – from Cyprus, from Portugal, from Britain and of course from the West Indies. As a teenager I began thinking of myself as a person of the world – I was very multicultural in my outlook. As far as I was concerned beauty was in the eye of the beholder. If I saw a beautiful white girl, a beautiful black girl or a beautiful Indian girl it didn't matter to me. I looked in exactly the same way; honestly I did not even register what colour or culture they were.

Mercy Mercy Me is an incredibly emotional song for me that reminds me of growing

The amazing Marvin Gaye. ▶

"I'm sure Marvin is sitting up there thinking, I'm so pleased that my music has touched so many lives and so many hearts."

up in Leaside House in East London. Although it was a very multicultural estate the tolerance level wasn't as good as it should have been.

When I was eight years old I saw an incident with a young Jewish boy who was beaten up by a gang of black and white kids. It was on my way home from school and it made no sense to me, so much so that I began crying and thinking, so what if he's different? Why does he have to be beaten up? I asked my mum why it was happening and she tried to explain to me that the kids are idiots and not to worry. Later on when I was picked on for being black it made me feel how that Jewish boy felt.

Today it's Muslims or Eastern Europeans that have been singled out as being different. What does it matter what colour you are? Whether you are white, black, green or yellow it shouldn't matter. We need to embrace all cultures and enjoy the goodness of what they bring to life in Britain.

When I got a little older I got involved in situations where my friends were bullied at school and I would try to defend them or help them. I was never able to understand why some people like to bully others. As I've become older, and hopefully wiser, I can see that it's often about shortcomings and inadequacies within the person doing the bullying that motivates them. They are the weak ones, not the person who is being bullied.

For me life is about standing tall, trying to be happy and making the most of whatever talents you've been given and at the same time looking out for your loved ones and your friends.

And so Marvin's message still resonates 40 years on; it is still powerful and I believe it will transcend time. In a hundred years from now or as long as there is prejudice about colour or any other point of difference that sets people apart, Marvin's message will remain important and relevant. He is an absolute icon for his understanding and determination to see his album released. In fact *What's Going On* may never have seen the light of day if he wasn't a strong man. I think it's fair to say that it is probably the most influential album ever written.

I'm on a day out with my good friends Catherine, Joe and Richard in Margate. Who said facial hair ain't cool? ▲

With my mum after she passed her midwifery exams. ▶

Mercy **Mercy Me** (The Ecology)
Written by Marvin Gaye in 1966

It made No.4 on the *Billboard* Hot 100 Singles in America but failed to chart in the UK.

This was the second single to be taken from *What's Going On* and it made No.1 on the R&B charts before crossing over to the pop charts. Marvin's previous single from the album was the title track that also topped the American R&B charts and made No.2 on the *Billboard* chart. While neither of these two songs made the UK singles chart, *Save The Children* from the same album was a minor hit in 1971. While the album has become a favourite of so many, it failed to chart in Britain, but it did make No.6 in America.

Marvin Gaye had topped the UK singles chart in 1969 with *I Heard It Through the Grapevine* – a far more traditional Motown record. It was followed by *Too Busy Thinking About My Baby* and *Abraham, Martin and John* which both made the Top 10 in the UK during the following 12 months.

Born in 1939 Marvin's career had begun in the late 1950s as a member of the Moonglows, a doo-wop group from Washington D.C., his hometown. He signed to Motown in 1960 and his first job was as a drummer on the road for Smokey Robinson's Miracles. As a singer Gaye always veered towards jazz rather than straight ahead R&B that was Motown's staple and it often caused problems between the singer and Berry Gordy who owned Motown.

Gaye's first Motown hit was in 1962 and his first single of real note was *How Sweet It Is (To Be Loved By You)* in 1964. Over the next three years he had a lot of success with duets, singing with people including the gifted singer Tammi Terrell. *What's Going On* was a radicle departure for Motown and for Marvin Gaye but it sealed his reputation.

Marvin had long-running struggles with drugs and depression during his life before being shot dead in 1984, the day before his 45th birthday, by his father. Marvin had intervened in an argument between his parents. A tragic end to a troubled life of one of the 20th century's most gifted vocalists.

Marvin Gaye. ◄

Let's StayTogether

Andy's influence – **Al Green**

Let's Stay Together for me personifies the human spirit of one woman – my mother. She has been so influential in my life and sadly she's no longer with us. For me the message in this song is all about the huge human spirit that my mother had, which in part was an automatic responsibility of giving birth to three kids, the responsibility of nurturing us through the good and the bad times, the happy and sad times, and never once wavering.

From the day I was born she couldn't hold me as I was in an incubator, nor could she for the ten months I was in hospital. During this time she visited me every day to see how I was getting along, all the while desperate to take me home. Much later she would say to me, "Andrew, I used to walk Coppetts Wood for you; I could have been mugged, raped or anything! And then where would you be?" This was when I was getting on her nerves as a teenager; with the benefit of hindsight I now think she was probably looking at me and being reminded on a daily basis of the man she had lost.

Mum's marriage to my stepfather ended when I was about 15 or 16; at the time I was a bit of a handful. I wasn't really bad but I was not acting responsibly, of course at that age I did not really understand what my mum was going through. I was constantly disappearing, staying at mates' houses for six or seven days at a time. I think now I was trying to find myself, whereas Mum definitely knew more about me than I knew about myself. She found it hard to understand me, but she never once failed to be supportive of me or my brother and sister. And while I was trying to find myself, Mum was working as a nurse, caring for old people.

Now, whenever I think of my mum she makes me feel very strong and every time I hear *Let's Stay Together* it reminds me of her and just how amazing she was in holding our family together through the toughest of times. Mum proved her strength in many ways. When my stepfather wanted to take the house away from her she fought to keep it so we had a roof over our heads. Mum remortgaged the house and worked three jobs to keep the money coming in, all the while raising us kids in a way that made us better people.

Mum was so inspirational and I cannot speak too highly of her. Now I know just about

Al Green. ▶

"*Let's Stay Together* will always be my song about my mum."

everyone feels that way about their mother and I'm not trying to say she's better than anyone else's mum, but she had so much to contend with yet never weakened. Which isn't to say she was perfect! She could be so stubborn at times, but it was her stubbornness that gave her the determination to succeed.

It makes me sad because she's not here to experience the joys and the successes that I've had nor is she able to enjoy my family – her grandkids – and for them to be able to enjoy her and learn from her as they are growing up. What's really upsetting is that I didn't say those things to her when she was still around; it's something that other people have said to me about family and friends that they have lost. It's a lesson for all of us and I hope I never again fail to say the things that are important at the time, rather than waiting until it's too late.

I should have said to my mother that she did a great job; she made me grow up and understand the world. At the same time she understood that it was very much a give and take situation. What she taught me I'm trying very hard to teach my children and to teach them well. I miss her very dearly and I'm sure my brother and sister feel exactly the same way as I do.

Chillin' on a hot day in my beloved Arsenal shirt. ▲
Denise, Tara 4, Jacob 2, my mum and me with dyed peroxide hair, having a rest. ▶

Let's **Stay Together**

Written by Al Green, Willie Mitchell & Al Jackson Jr. in 1971

The song topped the *Billboard* Hot 100 in America and made No.7 in the UK singles chart.

Al Green's career began in his teens as a member of his family's singing quartet, which toured the South extensively. By the 1960s he had left the family band after listening to the wrong kind of music as far as his father was concerned. Aged 21 he recorded a solo single and three years later he recorded his debut record for Hi Records in Memphis under the guidance of the talented Willie Mitchell – a songwriter and producer.

His second album for Hi Records included the classic single, *Tired of Being Alone*, but it was his third album that really launched Al Green's career. *Let's Stay Together* was the name of the album as well as the hit single that helped establish his name. It was written by Green and Mitchell along with Al Jackson Jr. who was also the drummer with Booker T & the MGs. When the album came out, *Rolling Stone* magazine said, "Green's voice is something to marvel at. He can croon, shout, scat, rise to the smoothest falsetto, and throw in the funkiest growls." *Let's Stay Together* was also successfully covered by Tina Turner in 1983 and reached No.6 on the UK charts.

It was not long after this album came out that Al Green was attacked in his home by a lover with whom he was having an affair; she then committed suicide. Green, seeing it as a spiritual wake-up call turned to God, the church and gospel music. He became an ordained pastor and ran services at a church close to Elvis Presley's home, Graceland. Green returned to R&B music appearing on tours and TV. Al Green is a consummate soul singer who has been a huge influence to many singers, including Andy.

Tina Turner. ◀

Lean
OnMe

Andy's influence – **Bill Withers**

In 1975 our family moved to Penryn Street in Camden Town. It was one of those do-it-yourself moves, meaning I had to help Mum by lugging stuff out of the car and into our new home. At one point I had my head in the back of the car, sorting out what to carry in next, when I heard a voice behind me say, "Hello, are you moving in?" As I turned around I saw a young dark-haired lad who was wearing flares and boots; he was clutching a ball. "Do you want to play football?" "No I can't. I've got to help my mum with the moving in", to which the boy replied, "I've got a really hard shot, you know." He turned and walked off leaving me thinking, what has that got to do with anything? Little did I know that this was the start of a beautiful friendship.

I soon found out that the boy's name was Mario Andrea. He was a ten-year-old Cypriot (I was 11) and he lived opposite me. Mario became like a brother from another mother to me and his family became a second family; he introduced me to his distant cousins and friends, quickly making me an integral part of his life. In the process he became the first proper friend I had ever had. We liked the same type of music, especially black music, but he also loved rock – in fact he introduced me to all types of music.

At the same time he could be really cheeky and would get me into all kinds of trouble with my mum. As a result I would get extra jobs to do around the house,

Me back in my old stomping ground of Camden Market. ▶

especially washing up the dishes, which I hated. But from the start of our friendship if he was in any trouble he could lean on me for any help he ever needed in the same way as I could on him.

If Mario was having problems in his household then the two of us would find solace with each other. When we were in each other's company we didn't have to worry what was happening domestically. *Lean On Me* reminds me of this wonderful person – my teenage soul mate.

Don't get me wrong, there were times when I wanted to strangle him, but within the space of a couple of days we were back doing what we normally did – being silly and mischievous. By the time we were 15 and 16, Mario and I used to head south from Camden Town to the wild West End. We would go to Soho to play the slot machines and see the sights! While that was great fun it was depressing passing through the Kings Cross area seeing the prostitutes and the pimps at work. Some of the girls we knew from our own area. They had got into the wrong kind of company, started taking drugs and then ended up on the streets to pay for their habit; it was so sad, but at the same time all part of growing up.

We did our growing up together, an incredibly important time in anyone's life. We also worked together for ten and a half years. We had so many laughs and so much fun; we went on holidays together and we really were inseparable. If we were out gallivanting, and not going to our own homes, I would stay at his place or vice versa. If he needed money I was always there for him – I was his rock and he was mine. Mario was like the epicentre of all our friends; everyone would gather around Mario and he would bring us all together.

I can't describe the loss I felt when he passed away aged just 34 years old. It was as if a light had gone out, and not just for me. After he died our group of friends went off and did their own thing – his power that had brought us together was snuffed out. Later we began to get back together again and I'm lucky that the people I really class

Mario. ▲

as my friends have stayed with me even after what has happened following my *X Factor* success; there's been no animosity and no jealousy over what has happened to me.

I was so devastated after losing Mario that it came to a point where I nearly lost my family, and it was only the spirit of my wife Denise that brought me back to where I should be. Denise made me realise that I had to remember my friend in the right way and not in a way that was destructive to us.

In some ways I think it made it easier to deal with my mother's passing a few years later; I said to myself that I was never going to get that crazy, that out of sync, ever again. But I still so dearly miss him and *Lean On Me* will always be the song for Mario and Andy.

"It sums up the amount of effort we put into staying close as a family."

Me outside my friend's house in Charrington Street, Camden Town, posing with my boogie box, age 16. ▲

Lean **On Me**

Written by Bill Withers in 1972

Bill Withers' single topped the *Billboard* chart for three weeks in the summer of 1972 and made No.18 in the UK later in the year.

Bill Withers, the youngest of 13 children, was born in Slab Fork, West Virginia in 1938. After serving nine years in the US Navy, he moved to Los Angeles in 1970 where he lived in a rundown part of the city. He wrote *Lean On Me* as he missed the strong sense of community in which he had grown up. "I bought a little piano and I was sitting there just running my fingers up and down it. In the course of doing the music, that phrase crossed my mind, so then you go back and say, 'OK, I like the way that phrase, *Lean On Me*, sounds with this song.'"

Lean On Me became Withers' only No.1 in 1972 and is one of a very few songs that has topped the American charts in two different versions; the other was by Club Nouveau in 1987. Withers' version comes from his second album and his first album included another of his best-known songs, *Ain't No Sunshine*. Six years after *Lean On Me* was a British hit, Withers scored his biggest UK hit with *Lovely Day*, which reached No.7 in the charts. Twelve years later a remixed version of the same song made No.4 in the charts. It's the song in which Withers holds the note for what seems like an eternity – it is in fact 18 seconds.

After the 1970s Withers' career was steady, but there was not a return to the glory days, although he did win a Grammy, to add to the one he received for *Lean On Me*, for *Just The Two Of Us*, a song he recorded with jazz saxophonist Grover Washington Jr. These days Withers runs a music publishing company, which looks after his work – it must be lucrative as his songs appear frequently in TV commercials and are covered by other artists.

Bill Withers. ◄

IFoundLovin'

Andy's influence – The Fatback Band

I just love this song!

This song reminds me of the days of shiny shoes and me doing my dance moves, which back then were hip – now they might just be a little bit old hat! It was a wonderful time, as many of you will know. It was the era of 'soul weekenders' – listening to all those fabulous radio stations in London that played sweet soul music – a time of Robbie 'If it moves, Funk it' Vincent, the late Steve Walsh, Greg Edwards, who was born in Grenada and raised in New York, and of course Tony Blackburn.

There was so much great music back then, by artists that included Major Harris, Shalamar and Kool and the Gang with their anthemic soul records. I loved hearing great tunes on the radio and then heading off down to Groove Records or Red Records in search of the songs that became the soundtrack to my late teens and early twenties.

Just like any other guy of my age the testosterone was flying high, but at the time I was also a bit of a shy fella. I wasn't a player at all and for a long while I was always the one getting dumped by my girlfriends. Sometimes a girl wanted to rekindle whatever it was we had, but I usually thought, no, what's the point of going backwards.

I Found Lovin' always makes me think of the freedom of my youth, the ability to go anywhere, do anything and feel like the world was waiting for me. At that point in my life I felt I could be anything I wanted to be. There were so many clubs that we went to, clubs that played the greatest sounds for the gang of us that would go out together at the weekends, not a gang in the bad sense of the word, but a gang of mates just looking to have a fun time.

Usually come the end of the night we all had red tongues because we drank Pernod and blackcurrant all night. Sometimes, for a change, it was Southern

Soul legends, Kool and the Gang. ▶

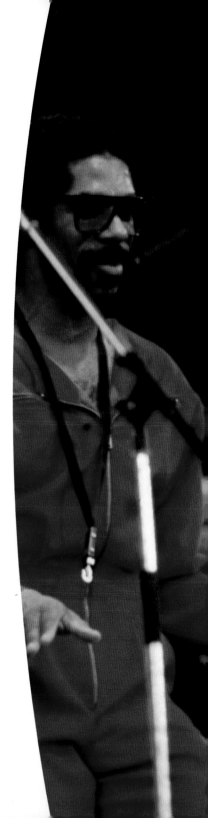

Comfort and lemonade, one too many of those and it made dancing a real challenge. The music that was coming out of America and Britain was not just a soundtrack to my life, it was also an inspiration to me. Besides those I've already mentioned there were Loose Ends, The SOS Band, William Bell, Steve Arrington, Philip Bailey, Change, Luther Vandross, Breakwater, Al Hudson, George Duke, Alexander O'Neal, The Brothers Johnson and René & Angela.

There was also Beggar & Co, with their amazing horn section, and founder members of Light of the World, a group whose record, *London Town*, just summed it all up for me – "London Town, pretty girls everywhere." They were very much a part of my growing up and remind me of my brother, my cousins and his friends who I was forever trying to tag along with; they were a bit older than me and didn't want a 'kid' hanging around cramping their style. If you've not heard any of the albums by Light of the World they are brilliant; they will instantly tell you what my young life was like.

The fact is my list of influential music is so long that I could go on and on. These artists were just some that I loved and they were what inspired me to sing. It was especially bands like Light of the World and Loose Ends that were showing me the way as they were British artists doing R&B that proved to me you did not have to be an American to sing soul music.

As well as all the upbeat soul songs, there were all those great 'slow jams'; the songs that at the end of a night became the opportunity to get on the dance floor for that slow groove with a girl that you had spotted. My mates and me would be eyeing each other dancing close with the girls – we'd all have smiles on our faces. If we were very lucky the reward would be a phone number at the end of the evening. Sometimes that might even lead to a date. As the song by Chic says, these really were "Good Times" and *I Found Lovin'* is the song I've chosen to remember, when London really was a 'Soul City'.

> "I was such a lover of UK soul. Those records were such an important part of my growing up."

Posing with my old friends John Vitorino & Pascoe, showing-off the six pack I once had. Shame about the boxers though! ▶

53

I Found **Lovin'**

Written by Johnny Flippin & Mike Walker in 1983

The Fatback Band made No.49 on the UK singles chart in June 1984 and in 1987 a remix made No.7 on the charts; it failed to chart in America.

The Fatback Band started life in New York City in 1970 having been put together by drummer Bill Curtis who was inspired by the fatback jazz sound of New Orleans to create a unique funk sound for a new generation of fans. The band, that included Johnny Flippin on bass who co-wrote *I Found Lovin'*, had their first US hit in 1973 with *Street Dance* before going on to have another 11 hits on the American R&B charts over the coming four years, of which *Spanish Hustle* was the best known.

In May 1978 the band finally cracked the Top 10 of the R&B charts with *I Like Girls*. During this period they never once made the *Billboard* Hot 100. In 1980 they had their biggest hit on the R&B charts with *Backstrokin'*.

The Fatback Band had their biggest UK single success with *Spanish Hustle* which made No.10 on the charts, that is until *I Found Lovin'* came along as a remix in 1987. Their 1979 single, *King Tim III (Personality Jock)* is now considered to be one of the first ever rap records. While their success was never huge they are considered by many to be one of the seminal groups within the modern R&B crossover movement and they certainly left their mark on Andy and many other young Londoners who trooped to seaside resorts in Britain for the 'soul weekenders' – events that are still going strong today at resorts like Prestatyn and Caister.

The Fatback Band. ◀

As

Andy's influence – Stevie Wonder

For me Stevie Wonder epitomises what a person with a disability can achieve. He's a shining light for people who have either been born blind or, like Stevie, lost their sight at a very young age. His heightened sense of touch, hearing and his imagination are amazing and the way he uses his imagination both lyrically and musically is an inspiration. Listen to the lyrics of *As* and you'll see exactly what I mean.

He's written so many songs that are full of beautiful imagery, words that are more poetry than just simple lyrics. He started out at Motown as Little Stevie Wonder, the year before I was born, and I'm sure back then that no one thought he would develop into the artist he has become. He was lucky to have been at Motown, to work with the Funk Brothers constructing music of all kinds that helped him develop as a musician and a lyricist.

For me Stevie Wonder is one of the greatest vocalists of all time. Stevie, Marvin Gaye and Donny Hathaway have everything – they have it all. There isn't a single soul singer that hasn't been influenced by Stevie's music; it's amazing how charismatic he can be behind a piano – his movements, his phrasings, his style and his vocal ability. I'm just happy to have been around in Stevie's era, to have seen him perform, watched him live and simply enjoyed his genius. There will never be another one like him.

Stevie Wonder's *As* is the perfect song for the perfect love affair. You will not be surprised then to know that this is a very special song for me. Out of all the love songs I've ever heard it's the one that is most perfect; I feel like it's my love song. Mario and me loved to go clubbing and I would see Denise at a place called Arizonas in Camden Town; we used to go to the same clubs including HQ's and Electric Ballroom. Later Denise told me that the first thing Mario said to her when things were getting a bit serious between us was "Denise don't break his heart". It was this that probably cemented our relationship as she knew I must be serious about her.

Denise and I have always been into music and we love hip hop, garage, soul, and R&B – as the O'Jays' song says, I love music… We love music!

Stevie Wonder. ▶

"When I think about writing the perfect song then I think of this as my inspiration."

While Stevie writes great melodies it's his lyrics that really grab me. As a singer it's important for me to have lyrics that really mean something, words that I can relate to, interpret and deliver with honesty and integrity. Let's face it, without words we wouldn't need singers!

I'm forever saying to Denise that if I was going to write a poem for her, *As* would be the perfect way to express how I feel. "As around the sun the earth knows she's revolving. And the rosebuds know to bloom in early May. Just as hate knows love's the cure. You can rest your mind assure that I'll be loving you always."

To be able to write lyrics like that is genius. *As*, as a love poem, gets to the heart of the matter of what it means to be in love with somebody. It tells them that you're there for life, that they're the number one person, the one you want to spend your life with. Stevie paints a picture and I hope I'm painting one too. Denise, this one's for you… thank you very much Stevie.

Here's me getting cosy with my girlfriend, who is now my wife, Denise – I had a thing about hats. ▶

As

Written by Stevie Wonder in 1976

It made No.36 on the US charts (1977), but did not chart in Britain.

As comes from Stevie's 1976 double album, *Songs in the Key of Life* that topped the US album charts and made No.2 in Britain – it was far from an unlucky 13th album.

Stevie Wonder, born Steveland Morris, was signed to Motown in 1961 as an 11 year old. It was Motown that gave him his name and released his first record later that same year, which became a hit in the label's hometown of Detroit. Two years later Little Stevie Wonder as he had become known, was topping the US charts with his live recording of *Fingertips (Pt2)*.

He had his next hit three years later, having dropped 'Little' from his name. *Uptight* made No.3 on the US charts and became his first British hit. For the remainder of the 1960s Stevie had hit after hit in America and Britain. His biggest UK successes came with *For Once in My Life* and *Yester-Me, Yester-You, Yesterday*.

Stevie was born six weeks prematurely and went blind as a baby when his retinas became detached. This in no way hampered his development as a singer, songwriter or as a musician. Initially known for his harmonica and drum playing, on his debut hit Stevie taught himself to play piano and with the advent of synthesisers in the early 1970s it allowed Stevie to break away from the strictures of what he saw as the Motown formula to record the ground-breaking album, *Music of my Mind*. It was not a big hit at the time as it failed to make the US album Top 20 but it pointed the way forward. From this point on Stevie developed as one of (soul) music's greatest songwriters.

Talking Book, Innervisions and *Fulfillingness' First Finale* were the albums that led up to *Songs in the Key of Life*, with the last two topping the US album charts. *As* was the fourth single taken from *Songs in the Key of Life* and it did not do as well as the previous three; *I Wish* and *Sir Duke* both topped the US singles chart and were Top 6 in the UK.

Stevie Wonder has won over 20 Grammy Awards, the most ever won by a solo artist, has had countless Top 10 records around the world and has inspired so many performers, both black and white; Stevie Wonder has done it all. His live shows are a tour de force and his reputation as a musical legend is secure for as long as people love great music.

Stevie in 2011 at the Martin Luther King Memorial. ◀

You Were
MeantForMe

Andy's influence – Donny Hathaway

When we were first together, Denise and I didn't have a special song, but we do now – Donny Hathaway's, *You Were Meant For Me*. It was not until we got married that this became an especially important song for us. For our wedding reception I roped in a good friend of mine to play guitar so that I could sing this to her. I think Denise liked it, at least I think that's what she was indicating when she started to cry while I was singing it to her. It definitely brought the house down and I have to admit it was the kind of reaction I was hoping for. It explains everything I feel about her in a way that I could not articulate nearly so well as it does through the lyrics of this beautiful song.

It was one of the hardest performances, if you can call it that, of my life. Not because Denise was making it difficult, but because my son, Jacob, who was high on too many fizzy, sugar laden drinks, was doing caterpillar moves across the floor as I was trying to be serious and romantic.

We were engaged for about ten years before Denise finally took it upon herself to organise our wedding, a very, very hot, 21st June, the longest day of the year. Along with the birth of my kids it is probably the greatest moment of my life.

We've been together for 20 years and we're still strong and just as in love as we've always been, possibly even more so. Denise is the reason why I'm having the success that I am; she's always really believed in me and along with my mum she has been the most important influence on my life.

As a child I saw the negative side of a relationship between my mother and my stepfather as he tried to dominate her; it was everything that could be wrong between a man and a woman. Even as a young kid I instinctively knew that this was not how it should be. By the time I got to my teens I began to understand that if a woman wanted to commit her life to me, and especially if she was to have my children, then she would need respect from me, a level of commitment that was the most that I could give. It's why this song was just so perfect for our wedding; it was the perfect song for the perfect occasion.

Donny Hathaway. ▶

"Denise is always asking me to play or sing this song for her."

Donny Hathaway has been an incredible influence in my life and vocally he's my favourite singer. He really touches me, both spiritually and in the way he interprets songs, as well as the actual notes he uses that make him totally unique, and yet most people have never really heard of him. Those that have will probably have done so because of the duets he sang with Roberta Flack – classics that include, *The Closer I Get to You* and *Where Is The Love*.

The sad thing is that Donny was a troubled man who in the end committed suicide. Along with Marvin Gaye he's one of the greatest losses we've had in soul music. Much as I love Stevie Wonder it is Donny Hathaway I admire most as a singer; his vocal delivery has taught me so much. The way he gets inside a song and makes the lyrics work so beautifully. Just listen to the words on this song and you will know why I sang it for my wife and I hope I have done justice to what is such a romantic song.

I hope I will get the chance to sing many more of his songs, as I believe they deserve to be heard by a wider audience. I know that at 46 years old there have been so many songs that have helped shape me, mould me and made me the person and the singer that I am. I believe that music reaches far deeper than just being something that simply entertains us, that makes us feel happy or even sad sometimes. Music really teaches us things about life on so many different levels.

If I had to narrow it down to just one song that I could take with me to that mythical desert island it would be *You Were Meant For Me* by Donny Hathaway – for a start it would make my wife happy and I always want to make her happy… and I hope, proud of me.

Denise and I fancied a cuddle in the Australian Outback. We were on holiday just before I entered *The X Factor*. ▶

You Were **Meant For Me**

Written by William (Pete) Peterkin in 1978

Donny Hathaway made No.17 on the American R&B charts with this song in 1978. It failed to dent the US Hot 100 or the British charts.

Donny Hathaway was born in Chicago in 1945 and was brought up by his grandmother. His musical awakening, like many other black American performers, occurred when singing in the church choir. After graduating from Howard University in Washington he worked as a songwriter, session musician and producer.

He recorded his first single under his own name in 1969 and it was in 1970 that he cracked the US *Billboard* singles chart with *The Ghetto part 1*. More hits followed before he recorded *Where Is The Love* with Roberta Flack that went to No.1 on the R&B chart and No.5 on the Pop chart in 1972. Over the next six years more hits followed, although none were big hits and nothing he ever released in Britain other than his duets with Flack ever became a hit.

In 1978 *The Closer I Get to You* was another R&B No.1 record and it got to No.2 on the *Billboard* Hot 100. Both this and *Where Is The Love* were minor British hits and it was not until after Hathaway's untimely death that he had a significant British hit when *Back Together Again* made No.3 in 1980.

Hathaway struggled with depression and paranoid schizophrenia for much of his adult life and it was after a recording session, working on new songs with Roberta Flack in January 1979, that he jumped from the 15th floor window of his Essex House apartment in New York City. It's not just Andy who respects Donny's work. In her song *Rehab*, Amy Winehouse mentioned him by name.

Donny Hathaway also sang with Roberta Flack. ◀

Ain't No
Stoppin' UsNow

Andy's influence – McFadden & Whitehead

Ain't No Stoppin' Us Now most definitely epitomises the sound of Philadelphia for me. Have I ever been to Philadelphia to hear what it sounds like? Well, no, but what I mean by this is the sound of Philadelphia International Records, the Philly Sound. While it was Gene McFadden and John Whitehead who co-wrote this song, it's the production values and the whole vibe that was created by the legendary production team of Gamble and Huff that does it for me. I just love the great big sound they had on so many of their records; *Ain't No Stoppin' Us Now* is an anthem for me and for tens of thousands of people who enjoyed the soul scene back in the late 1970s and early 1980s.

Kenny Gamble and Leon Huff to me are legendary figures in not just soul music but the whole of music and I know I'm not alone in thinking this. With that in mind you can begin to imagine how I felt in 2006 when I was asked to sing at the Ivor Novello Awards at which Gamble and Huff were given an International Achievement Award. I cannot think of two more deserving people and for me it really was a dream come true to be able to share the same stage with two of my musical heroes.

The two men started Philadelphia International Records in 1971, and have had so many hits along the way, creating some stone cold soul classics. Included among the many hits they have had there's been: *If You Don't Know Me By Now* by Harold Melvin & The Blue Notes, *Love Train* and *Back Stabbers* by The O'Jays, *TSOP* by MFSB and there was that other song, what was it now, oh yes, *Me and Mrs Jones* that was originally done by Billy Paul. Between them, they have produced over 175 gold and platinum records and without their fantastic music my teenage years would have been a whole lot less interesting.

I was invited to sing at the party after the Ivor Novello Awards ceremony and I chose five Gamble and Huff songs to perform. In the build-up I was just so excited to be doing it, but the closer it got to the actual evening of the gig the more nervous I became. On the way into London I was really quite scared thinking about the people that I was about to meet.

Kenny Gamble (right) and Leon Huff at the Ivor Novello Awards. ▶

"I see these songs as soul songs, in the way that they've all had a profound effect on me."

Once I actually got up on stage and started to sing, my nerves quickly evaporated and I concentrated, as I always do, on giving a good show. While I was singing I couldn't help but sneak a peak at Mr Gamble and Mr Huff who, along with their entourage, were watching my performance, at least it seemed to me anyway, very intently. After I finished singing they were brought up on stage to make a speech. After saying a few words of introduction Kenny Gamble turned and looked at me and said, "Boy, you can sing!" It was all said in that deep, husky, quiet, yet authoritative voice. I just thought to myself, imagine being in the studio and having him speak to you like that. That reassuring voice of such a musical legend would give you so much confidence to perform to the very best of your ability. It was one of those moments that will live with me for the rest of my days.

At the Ivor Novello Awards the last song I performed was *Ain't No Stoppin' Us Now*, which was a great song to close with, and I have to say it brought the house down. Man oh man, life is good, is what I thought to myself as I came off stage. Who would have thought as a result of being on a TV talent show that I, a dude from North London in his forties, would be singing for his musical heroes. On top of my platinum album it really was the icing on the proverbial cake. It still makes me smile just thinking about it now.

Me performing on *The X Factor* live tour at Manchester's MEN Arena in February 2006, a few months before my appearance with Gamble and Huff. ▶

Ain't No **Stoppin' Us Now**

Written by Jerry Cohen, Gene McFadden & John Whitehead in 1979

It spent a week at No.1 on the R&B chart and made No.13 on the *Billboard* Hot 100, as well as making No.5 on the UK singles chart.

The song was written by McFadden, Whitehead and their keyboard player Jerry Cohen and was taken from their self-titled debut album in 1979. After nearly a decade of hits from the label that had been started by Kenny Gamble and Leon Huff this was one of their last major successes as a single release.

McFadden and Whitehead had formed a group called The Epsilons in the 1960s that toured with Otis Redding after which the duo signed to Philadelphia International Records shortly after the label began, although it was as songwriters that they were initially successful. Their first big hit was *Back Stabbers* for The O'Jays in 1972. They also worked with Teddy Pendergrass, Harold Melvin & The Blue Notes, James Brown, Stevie Wonder, Lou Rawls and Archie Bell & The Drells before having their worldwide hit with *Ain't No Stoppin' Us Now* that has sold in excess of 7 million copies.

Like so many other songs with a message of positive energy, *Ain't No Stoppin' Us Now* has been used in all sorts of contexts including being the theme song for boxer Larry Holmes and being played at the 2008 Democratic Party Convention when Barack Obama accepted the nomination as their presidential candidate.

Tragically both men are now dead. Whitehead was shot dead by two gunmen in 2004 while working on his car outside his Philadelphia home. It's believed to be a case of mistaken identity and the murder remains unsolved. Whitehead was 54 years old. In 2006 McFadden died of cancer; he was 57 years old.

McFadden & Whitehead. ◄

Me
AndMrsJones

Andy's influence – Billy Paul

Me and Mrs Jones changed my whole life.

It's incredible when I look back and think to myself what my life was like before *X Factor*. I was settled – a family man with lovely kids and a lovely wife. I did not have to exert myself too much, with no more excitement in my life than a trip to the Emirates to watch the Arsenal. Then all of a sudden my wife decided to enter me into this competition, a competition she had seen on the TV the previous year that she thought could be just the thing for me.

I have to say that Denise did a great job on me – convincing me that I should do it, and more to the point I could do it, and although I was initially reluctant she never stopped believing in me – believe you me Denise can be very persuasive and persistent. Very quickly events seemed to take over my life and before I knew where I was I was on the television. It was such a thrill, especially as people seemed to like what they heard.

This was – if you remember – the second series of *The X Factor*; it was 2005 and I laid out my stall in the very first week by singing *The Greatest Love of All,* which I still think was my best performance of the series. Over the coming month I performed songs by The Real Thing, Nat King Cole, Andy Williams, Boyz II Men and then in week six I sang my 'game-changer' – not that I necessarily thought it would be at the time.

The idea for *Me and Mrs Jones* came from the lovely Kate Thornton and I will be forever grateful to her for reminding me of such a great song. My initial thought was could I pull it off? It is after all an iconic song, a memorable song that Billy Paul had made his own, with more than a little help from Kenny Gamble and Leon Huff.

In the build-up to the show Mark Hudson, my vocal coach, was very pleased with the way I sang it, but rehearsals are one thing and are totally different to the live show. When it came to the actual show itself I felt as if I was transported back to the days of the Philadelphia Sound. It felt like The O'Jays, Harold Melvin & The Blue Notes, The Three Degrees and all those other great acts that Gamble and Huff produced, were looking out for me.

Billy Paul. ▶

"I did it for my wife, my kids and all the guys that have a dream."

On that Saturday night in November I walked on stage wearing a light grey suit and white shirt and everything felt just right. I just hit the groove and when it finished all I can remember is this wall of sound coming at me from the audience and Simon Cowell saying, "I absolutely loved that. I wish I was looking after you." It was the moment that really changed people's perception of me; it also showed that a mature singer could cut it in a competition that was essentially aimed at younger people. That week I topped the vote for the first time.

The one thing I've never done and I really want to do is to be able to properly thank Kate Thornton for her suggestion. To a singer like me the right choice of song is so important because when all is said and done artists may come and artists may go, but songs will always be there and great songs leave legacies and none more so than *Me and Mrs Jones* from an era of great soul music.

When I performed at the Ivor Novello Awards for Gamble and Huff *Me and Mrs Jones* was naturally one of the five songs I did along with *Ain't No Stoppin' Us Now, If You Don't Know Me By Now, When Will I See You Again,* and *Back Stabbers*. So for me it kind of completed the journey and took me full circle from being a fan of the two legendary producers, and this fabulous song, through the life-changing experience of *The X Factor,* to performing it in tribute

My mother and Denise getting cosy. ▲

to them. It really was a magic moment for me getting to meet them both and it could only have been bettered if Billy Paul had been there too.

In the end of course I did not win *The X Factor,* I was beaten, just, by Shayne Ward who got 1.2% more of the vote than I did. Of course I was gutted not to have won. After a journey of ten weeks it would have been lovely to have done it, but I do not look back with anything other than joy in my heart for having been given the opportunity, even if Denise did have to twist my arm. I met so many fantastic people and learned so much and my life really did change forever on 19th November 2005 when I sang *Me and Mrs Jones* for that first time. And today I wouldn't change a thing.

Except for one thing. While I was on *X Factor* my mum became seriously ill. My mum, who was so brilliant at keeping the family together with her old-school discipline, knew that I had got onto the programme but just as the series began, she went into hospital and never came out. Each week through the euphoria of doing well with my singing I had to visit the hospital to watch my mum being given different treatments in an effort to keep her alive. Sadly they failed and my mum passed away.

Throughout all this Denise, my brother, sister and my kids helped to keep me together but so did three other people: Kate Thornton, Sharon Osbourne and Simon Cowell showed serious concern for me and were absolutely brilliant throughout the series. I will never ever have anything bad to say about those guys and in fact I want to go on record to say what wonderful, kind and caring people they were to me.

And so I remember when there was a time that I was just a guy with a good voice, but a guy with a dream. I was also a guy with a wife with the vision to allow my dream to become reality.

My children Tara & Jacob with my brother Bertrand's kids Karl, Josh & Myles at my mum's house in Grenada in 2005. I had to fly out there after Saturday's *X Factor* show to bury Mum. I stayed for four days and headed back for dress rehearsals on the Thursday. It was a very difficult time. ▲

From left to right: 2005 *X Factor* contestants Richie, Haifa, Chico, Maria, Brenda & me outside the hotel we stayed at in LA, during the last auditions before the live shows.

Me and *Xtra Factor* presenter Ben Shephard at Sharon Osbourne's LA mansion.

Posing outside Sharon's mansion in LA before being allowed inside.

With the lovely Kate Thornton who was so welcoming.

The gorgeous Sharon Osbourne with PR guru Gary Farrow in LA during the *X Factor* auditions.

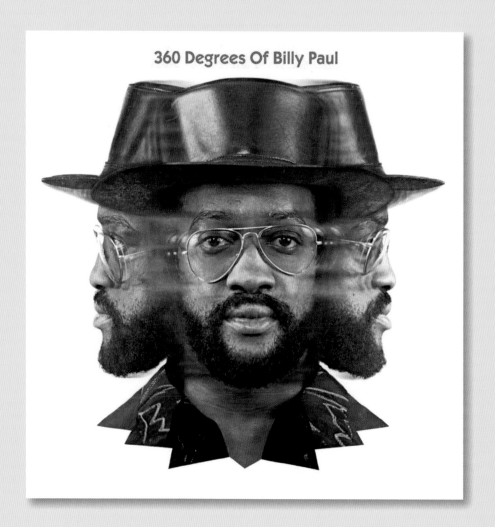

360 Degrees Of Billy Paul

Me and **Mrs Jones**

Written by Cary Gilbert, Kenny Gamble & Leon Huff in 1972

Billy Paul's original version of the song made No.1 on the *Billboard* Hot 100 singles chart for three weeks in December 1972. As well as topping the US R&B charts it made No.12 in the UK in 1973.

Recently Kenny Gamble explained how this classic song came about. He and Leon Huff got the idea while sitting in a bar beneath the Schubert Building in Philadelphia where their office was located. "This guy used to come into the bar every day – little guy that looked like a judge. The next day he came in again, and every day after he'd come in, this girl would come in 10-15 minutes after he'd get there, and they'd sit in the same booth, then go to the jukebox and play the same songs. We said, 'That's me and Mrs Jones.' Then, when they'd get ready to leave, he would go his way and she would go hers. It could have been his daughter, his niece, anybody, but we created a story that there was some kind of romantic connection between these people, so we went upstairs to our office and wrote the song." And what a song!

Like all the great songs it paints a lyrical picture that when added to the melody conjures up that special something that we can all feel, and some people can even relate to it. Cary Gilbert, the other name on the song's credits, is a lyricist who frequently worked with Gamble and Huff.

After army service Billy Paul who was born Paul Williams briefly became one of Harold Melvin's Blue Notes before Gamble and Huff produced his debut album in 1968. Two years later the follow-up album sold locally but did nothing for Paul's career on a wider scale. A third album the following year began to garner interest but it was with the release of *Me and Mrs Jones* that his reputation was made.

Billy Paul's career never again scaled the heights of *Me and Mrs Jones* but his silky soulful voice graced many excellent records including a cover of Paul McCartney's *Let 'em In* in 1976 and Elton John's *Your Song* the following year. And that was just about it as far as hits were concerned from Billy Paul, but he will always be remembered for this song.

Billy Paul's *360 Degrees Of Billy Paul.* ◀

ItWasYou

I wanted this album to be not just songs from the past that I like to sing, even when they are very personal, but new material too and so when I started working with Eliot on this project I said I would love to have the chance of recording some of his songs. He is such an accomplished songwriter who has written for Aretha Franklin, Mary J Blige, Take That and Bryan Adams among many others so it is a privilege to sing these two songs by Eliot.

When I sat down with Eliot in his studio we just talked about the music that I love and what inspires me. To begin with we had an even longer list of covers. When it came to picking the new songs for the album Eliot, knowing my love of soul music, played me four or five of his songs and these two were the ones I decided to record. I loved both of them the moment I first heard them.

My inspiration when writing this song was thinking of a guy at the end of a long life telling the angels what he remembered most. While he rattles off a list of things that he remembers he comes to the inevitable conclusion that It Was You… The message in this song is to be thankful for what you have, not what you covet.

Eliot Kennedy

When You Love
Someone

I hope these songs give you an indication of what is coming next – another album full of new material. I'm writing some of my own songs with other writers that are giving me the chance to express myself. These two songs are a pointer to my future…

To me they fit right into the feel and the vibe of the album as a whole and while they are new songs they have a feel of songs from the golden era of soul. To me the album makes complete sense, it tells the story of my life, and while there's no end to it, these songs help to bring my life bang up-to-date.

This is a song about how brilliant it is to be in love. Everything is more colourful, the sunshine's brighter, the world is more beautiful and you want to shout out the name of the one you love. It's all about heightened awareness. Love is what helps the world to turn more smoothly. Don't you just love it?

Eliot Kennedy

1. For the Good Times • (Kris Kristofferson) Universal Music Careers ℗ 1970

2. Born Free • (John Barry & Don Black) Sony/ATV Music Publishing ℗ 1966

3. Mercy Mercy Me (The Ecology) • (Marvin Gaye) EMI April Music Inc ℗ 1971

4. Let's Stay Together • (Al Green, Al Jackson Jr & Willie Mitchell) Al Green Music Inc/Al Jackson Jr Music/ Irving Music Inc ℗ 1971

5. Lean On Me • (Bill Withers) Interior Music Corp ℗ 1972

6. I Found Lovin' • (Johnny Flippin & Michael Walker) Takein Care of Business Music Inc ℗ 1983

7. As • (Stevie Wonder) Black Bull Music Inc/Jobete Music Co Inc ℗ 1976

8. You Were Meant For Me • (William (Pete) Peterkin) WB Music Corp ℗ 1978

9. Ain't No Stoppin' Us Now (Jerry Cohen, Gene McFadden & John Whitehead) Warner-Tamerline Publishing Corp ℗ 1979

10. Me and Mrs Jones (Kenny Gamble, Leon Huff & Cary Gilbert) Warner-Tamerline Publishing Corp ℗ 1972

11. It Was You (Eliot Kennedy) Sony/ATV Music Publishing ℗ 2011

12. When You Love Someone (Eliot Kennedy) Sony/ATV Music Publishing ℗ 2011

Produced by Eliot Kennedy and James Jayawardena for BearBone Productions.

Engineered and mixed by James Campbell.

Recorded and mixed at Steelworks Studios, Sheffield, UK.

Keyboards – James Jayawardena

Drums – Gareth Brown

Bass – Vinzenz Benjamin

Guitars – Jonny Heyes

Sax – Steve Beighton

Trumpet – Ed Collins

Trombone – Ron Christlow

Backing Vocals – Nicole Russo, Philippa Hanna, Kat Eaton & Eliot Kennedy

Mercy Mercy Me (The Ecology) features FaithChild on the rap.

Faith, loyalty, trust, belief, vision, courage, friendship, passion, knowledge and direction are all needed if there is to be success. It's my album, but it would not have happened without all these ingredients that the following people have contributed so generously in so many different ways. So it's a big thank you from me to all of you.

A very special thank you to the Hayes family John & Donna (true life long friends), Matt & Laura, Sophia, Louisa, Roxy and Jack – you came along when we needed you.

A massive thank you also has to go to a very special man and new true friend, Eric Herd. I truly appreciate all you have done for Denise and I.

Champions (UK) Plc my management company, Amelia Benskin, Victoria Marconetto, Jodie Barker, Jennifer Johnson, Catherine Goss, Benoit Lawrence, Oliver Willson, Rebecca Whalley, Rebecca Morrell and Sarah Garner for all your support and the hard work to make this album possible.

A huge thank you to E J Entertainments Ltd for allowing me to make this album, and also allowing it to be so personal.

To all at Steelworks Studios – I can't wait to start the next one; Eliot Kennedy and James Jayawardena, you are the A-List of producing and songwriting. There's nothing you can't do. I call you my musical Superheroes and the brains behind the album; you have everything an artist needs to enable them to reach the stars. James Campbell, you have the patience of a saint and are a great engineer. Thank you to all the musicians who helped me to make sweet music: Gareth Brown, Vinzenz Benjamin, Jonny Heyes, Steve Beighton, Ed Collins, Ron Christlow, Nicole Russo, Philippa Hanna, Kat Eaton, Eliot Kennedy and FaithChild.

Thank you Tony Wilkinson for getting all these important people around the table and being a vital member of the team.

Richard Havers, a true gentleman who understands how to bring words to life.

Thanks to Eliot for the M&M's and salted popcorn combo.

Brian Grant, your vision and experience in the world of filming & directing were invaluable to this project.

To Vanessa Gardner, Carl Edwards, Rebecca Ellis & Kevin Gardner at Instinctive; thank you for all your ideas, hard work and cooperation.

Anthony Stanley, thank you for all your creative input; you're a wonderful photographer and man.

Louise Page, you went beyond what was required of you; thank you so much (for the tie and shirt).

Steve Kyprianou, you are the rarest of human beings and I'm forever grateful you're in my life and my family's.

Amy Frankland, Beautiful Girl.

To all my family, Denise, Tara and Jacob Abraham, Bertrand, Dionne, Karl, Josh, Myles and Luke Gilbert Campbell, Judy Abraham, Stephen, Jayne, Halle and Annais Campbell.

To all of you, thank you for being part of my past and my present. I'm sure we'll make